One Short

Written by Dave Cousins

Illustrated by Helen van Vliet

Collins

Me and Jamie had been best friends for five years.
Now he was leaving.

2

I waved as the removals lorry disappeared into the distance, taking Jamie to a new house and a new school. Would he find a new best friend too?

On Monday at school, I had to sit next to an empty chair.

At break time I scored a brilliant goal and turned round to celebrate. Then I remembered Jamie wasn't there.

Lunchtime was worse. As usual, Dad had made me "surprise sandwiches". Jamie liked Dad's strange fillings, so we used to swap. Now I was on my own.

I took a bite ... marmalade and peanut butter. Disgusting!

On Tuesday morning somebody was sitting in Jamie's chair.

"Hello, I'm Daniel," said the new boy.

"That's Jamie's seat," I said, glaring at him.

At break, Daniel wanted to play football. We were one short without Jamie, but I shook my head.

"We don't need any more players," I said and ran outside with Matt.

Just because Daniel was sitting in Jamie's chair, it didn't mean he could take his place.

As the fifth goal went in against us, I spotted Daniel watching from the touchline. I tried to pretend he wasn't there.

But Daniel wouldn't leave me alone.
"What flavour?" he asked, pointing to
my sandwiches at lunchtime.

"Jam and tuna," I replied.

Daniel pulled a face. "Want one of mine?
They're chocolate spread."

"No thanks," I said, forcing down
another mouthful of sandwich.

On Wednesday night Jamie phoned. Hearing his voice made me feel happy ... and sad.

I told him about our terrible footy results.

"You need someone to take my place!" he said. I felt my cheeks go red.

13

Thursday was a total disaster. My egg and banana sandwiches smelt so bad that I threw them out of the canteen window. Of course, Mrs Stone chose that moment to walk past! I had to spend the rest of lunchtime picking up litter and missed the match.

I was chasing a crisp packet through
the playground when I saw Daniel, kicking
a ball against a wall by himself. He looked like
I felt.

By lunchtime the next day, I'd made up my mind. I saw Daniel heading for the school gates and ran after him.

"Wait!" I shouted. "We need you for the match!"

"I didn't think you wanted me," said Daniel, not stopping. "Anyway, I'm going to my nan's for lunch."

I'd messed everything up and now we were going to lose again.

"We're still one short," I said, running on to the pitch.

"No we're not!" Matt pointed over my shoulder.

I turned around and there was Daniel, standing in goal!

"Who needs lunch?" he said, grinning.

For the first time since Jamie left, we actually won!

"I'm starving now!" said Daniel as we walked off the field.

"I don't suppose you like fish paste and pickle sandwiches?" I said.

He grinned. "I'm so hungry, I'll eat anything!"

"Today could be your lucky day," I told him and I reached into my bag.

Making new friends

lonely
at lunchtime

not wanting
a new friend

missing Jamie

seeing that Daniel
is lonely as well

finding out that
Daniel wants to
be friends

enjoying a new
friendship

23

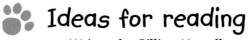

Ideas for reading

Written by Gillian Howell
Primary Literacy Consultant

Learning objectives: *(reading objectives correspond with Turquoise band; all other objectives correspond with Copper band)* read independently and with increasing fluency longer and less familiar texts; empathise with characters and debate moral dilemmas portrayed in texts; infer characters' feelings in fiction

Curriculum links: Citizenship, P.E.

Interest words: friends, removals, goal, celebrate, surprise, marmalade, peanut, touchline, flavour, chocolate

Resources: pens and paper

Word count: 507

Getting started

- Read the title together and discuss the cover illustration. Ask the children to look closely at the picture and suggest how the boy in the illustration is feeling. Ask them to suggest what the significance of the title is.

- Ask the children to read the back cover blurb together and discuss whether their first ideas about the story were right.

Reading and responding

- Read pp2–3 together. Point out the use of the first person narrator. Ask the children how they think the narrator is feeling.

- Ask the children to read the story aloud quietly to the end. Listen in as they read and prompt as necessary, e.g. on p4, if children struggle with *celebrate* explain that the *c* is a soft sound.

Returning to the book

- Turn to pp22–23 and ask the children to discuss how the narrator feels when he is missing his old friend and not prepared to meet anyone new, compared with how he feels once he decides to become friends with Daniel. Ask the children to put forward their own experiences when empathising with the narrator's emotions during these events.